MY HEART OF RICE

# MY HEART OF RICE

## A POETIC FILIPINO AMERICAN EXPERIENCE

ASHLEY C. LANUZA

NEW DEGREE PRESS
COPYRIGHT © 2020 ASHLEY C. LANUZA
All rights reserved.

MY HEART OF RICE
*A Poetic Filipino American Experience*

ISBN    978-1-64137-371-5  *Paperback*
        978-1-64137-281-7  *Kindle Ebook*
        978-1-64137-282-4  *Digital Ebook*

*To the manongs,*
*to the activists,*
*to the students,*
*to my family,*
*and to you.*

# CONTENTS

---

| | | |
|---|---|---|
| | **A NOTE FROM THE AUTHOR** | **13** |
| **1.** | **SPOONFUL OF LOVE** | **21** |
| | retelling | 22 |
| | nanay gloria's supermarket | 23 |
| | homework on the kitchen table | 24 |
| | dinner at seven p.m. part 1 | 25 |
| | dinner at seven p.m. part 2 | 25 |
| | our favorite | 26 |
| | birthday parties | 27 |
| | kamayan (hands) | 28 |
| **2.** | **YOUR COMIDA, MY VIDA** | **29** |
| | from sinaloa | 30 |
| | twisted tongues | 31 |
| | holding on to what I know | 32 |
| | three | 33 |
| **3.** | **PLAYGROUND PREJUDICES** | **35** |
| | kids on the playground | 36 |
| | the little differences | 37 |
| | rice versus beans | 38 |
| | unchanging | 39 |
| **4.** | **FILIPINO CLUB OF ONE** | **41** |
| | honorary latina | 42 |
| | one to none | 43 |
| | cultural exchange | 44 |
| | holding on a little less | 45 |

| | | |
|---|---|---|
| **5.** | **PARTYING PROTOTYPES** | **47** |
| | nothing i am | 49 |
| | lacking experience | 50 |
| | sophomore year | 51 |
| | birthday invites | 53 |
| **6.** | **LONGING FOR BELONGING** | **55** |
| | missing more than just friends | 56 |
| | letting go of what I know | 57 |
| **7.** | **COLLEGE-LEVEL DISCONNECT** | **59** |
| | your dream come true | 60 |
| | the lonely road | 61 |
| | not ready to go | 62 |
| | olvera street | 63 |
| **8.** | **UNIVERSITY OF UNLEARNING** | **65** |
| | recalling memories | 66 |
| | fitting in | 67 |
| | connecting unavailable | 68 |
| | presenting convictions | 69 |
| | defining the lines | 70 |
| **9.** | **FORGOTTEN HISTORIES** | **71** |
| | 1700s – Saint Malo Settlements of New Orleans, Louisiana | 73 |
| | shrimp paste | 74 |
| | 1904 – The Philippine Exhibition in St. Louis, Missouri | 75 |
| | the Philippine Question | 76 |
| | 1920s – Migrating Men of Stockton, California | 77 |
| | just like home | 78 |
| | only golden sunsets | 79 |
| | the good | 80 |
| | the bad | 81 |

| | |
|---|---|
| the american dream | 82 |
| exit signs | 83 |
| empty spaces | 84 |
| 1965 – Creation of the United Farm Worker's Association in Delano, California | 85 |
| please rise | 86 |
| united front | 88 |
| ¡si, kaya natin! | 89 |
| 1970s – Demolishing the International Hotel in San Francisco, California | 90 |
| the night of '77 | 91 |
| 1990s to Present – Overseas Filipino Workers | 92 |
| landline | 93 |
| cell phone | 94 |
| **10. COMMUNITY CONDITIONS** | **95** |
| hiya (noun) | 96 |
| stem | 97 |
| mental | 98 |
| unfair | 99 |
| utang na loob | 100 |
| intergenerational conflict | 101 |
| model minority | 102 |
| hive | 103 |
| in my silence | 104 |
| **11. IT'S THE LITTLE THINGS** | **105** |
| birthplace | 106 |
| enemy of the nation | 107 |
| american exotica | 108 |
| "it's not that serious" | 109 |
| to be | 110 |

**12. COMMON CONDITIONS** — **111**
- surnames — 112
- collectivist choices — 113
- to dads: — 114
- to moms: — 115
- degraded degrees — 116
- what they won't tell you — 117
- enforcing expectations — 118
- eyes on you — 119
- borders — 120
- no better — 122

**13. REBIRTH** — **123**
- lightning strike — 124
- this is filipino — 125
- broken perfection — 126
- hesitation — 127

**14. STUDENT ACTIVISM** — **129**
- self-led — 130
- self-investment — 131
- self-evaluation — 132
- self-awareness — 133
- self-criticism — 134

**15. FAR FROM THE FINISH LINE** — **135**
- lost in one place — 136
- finding space — 137
- undo the cliques — 138
- always redefining — 139

**16. TWO FLAGS ONLY** — **141**
- pueblo — 142
- abroad in Barcelona — 144
- present — 145

**17. CONVERSATIONS LOST IN TRANSLATION** **147**
    no questions, no answers      149
    awkward silence      150
    be quiet      151
    to: me      152
    hope and doubt      153

**18. WORK IN PROGRESS** **155**
    awakened      156
    claiming      157
    I am      158
    to lolocon:      160

**APPENDIX**      **161**

**REFERENCES**      **171**

**ACKNOWLEDGEMENTS**      **175**

# A NOTE FROM THE AUTHOR

---

"Where did you learn to cook?" I asked my grandfather with childlike curiosity.

The silver pot bubbled on the stove as sunset's orange-yellow beams flooded the stained countertop. Using the towel thrown carelessly over his shoulder, he wiped the sweat off his brow.

"Oh," Lolocon sighed, squinting at a memory only he could see. "In the Philippines, I was responsible for my seven younger siblings. I learned to cook to feed all of them. And now I just cook all the time."

He shrugged his shoulders in the humble way he always does, but I could see the ghost of a smile play on his lips. Lolocon rested his hand on his hip while stirring the aromatic pot of meat marinated in spices and sauces.

"Go finish your homework, na," he prodded, almost begging me to leave him alone, ladle in hand and proud of his stovetop creation.

I am starting where everything starts—home. Home is the foundation of all that we learn: love, comfort, tradition, and food. Food is such an integral part of home life because of the multisensorial way it satisfies our taste buds, appetites, relationships, and souls. The social power of food lies in its story, myth, or origin. Hot dogs mean baseball parks, buttered popcorn means movies, burgers mean American, and les escargots goes to the French. Food represents these different cultures, so, in a sense, we consume culture—literally.

When we consume culture, we determine our likes and dislikes, seeking more of what pleases us. During my travel abroad in Europe, I had an authentic German schnitzel platter consisting of breaded pork, mashed potatoes smothered with gravy, and a side of boiled, sweet red cabbage. The meal gave me a sense of the country's taste for hearty flavors that paired well with their love for refreshing beers. Moreover, I found I really liked the contrast of a sharp cabbage cutting through softened starches. I continued to search for the same experience I had when consuming that food because it made me content in a "sitting near the fire on a cold winter's day" type of way. (I found a similar experience in the Czech Republic, a country fond of its pilsner.) In consuming culture, we consume the knowledge offered to us. Thus, we deepen our understanding of ourselves and the world around us.

This is the story of my culture consumption, particularly my Filipino American culture. It begins with my grandfather,

Conrado, who toddler Ashley affectionately renamed "Lolocon." Lolo means "grandfather" in Tagalog, the major dialect of the Philippines, and "con" is short for his name. This book is a letter to him, about all the things I've come to understand about my cultural identity because of the cuisine he cooked every day.

My lolo and I are very close. After my parents separated, my mom was always working and I didn't see my dad on a daily basis. Lolocon was the one to drop me off and pick me up from after-school daycare, make sure I did my homework, and put me to bed. He's one of my favorite people on this Earth. Up until college, my grandfather cooked dinner for my immediate family on my mother's side. He cooked mostly Filipino food, including the well-known pancit and adobo and the less mainstream dishes like pinakbet and mechado. Each dish was served with rice. Each dish connected me to my Filipino heritage, along with the teleseryes (Filipino soap operas) we watched every night. Food was the consistent connection to my "Filipino-ness."

This chronological body of work starts at home, progresses into elementary, middle, and high school, and then into present-day college. It is an exploration of my "Filipino-ness" and what that means growing up in America, especially in neighborhoods not dominated by a Filipino demographic. It is about learning from these experiences that all started with food and the power food has in igniting self-discovery.

As a child, I attended parochial schools that were predominantly Hispanic. Elementary school was rife with microaggressions—little things said or done that I had bottled up. It's interesting and terrifying how much exclusivity and harm children can perpetuate without even knowing what they're doing or why they're doing it. Many kids eventually grow up to become educated and conscious individuals, but when a child is young, they are an unfiltered projection of the world around them. At a young age, how do children deal with cultural insensitivities and how do they affect children's future self-image?

High school was a culture shock when I found I was the only Filipino student in my class for most of the four years. I had difficulty fully relating to my Hispanic peers. However, I also had a bit of an edge because my former stepdad is from Mexico. I grew up speaking Spanish, consuming Mexican food, and connecting deeply with my abuelita. These influences brought up a lot of identity confusion. Because of my friendships and the adolescent need to socialize, I assimilated into Hispanic culture and reserved connecting with "Filipino-ness" for home. Although I am 100% Filipino, I think and speak like an American. I was never Mexican by blood, but I find strong comfort in Mexican communities. I even speak Spanish better than any Filipino language.

When my family, friends, and communities were so diverse, I questioned how I defined and presented myself. The cultural relationship—this gray area between Filipino, Mexican, and American cultures—is where I found the most confusion in piecing my identity together. This crisis encouraged me to seek a better understanding of my Filipino identity in college. This book is a result of those questions and the questions the search unveiled.

When I joined the Filipino organization on my college campus, I expected to make friends I could relate to and move on from there. But through student-led meetings and classes, I learned beyond relationships. I learned about what we call "community conditions," or issues observed within our communities that lead to internal and external conflict. For Filipino American communities, for instance, there is a lack of guidance when applying to American colleges because many applicants are children of recently migrated parents. I also learned a lot about Filipino American history, like the Filipino labor activists who helped start the United Farm Worker's Association with Cesar Chavez. Learning these histories was groundbreaking because they were never mentioned in my American history courses, even though they clearly occurred on American soil.

This organization also taught me about the nuances of identity in the Filipino community and how my identity differed from that of my family. I must clarify that there are differences between "Filipino" and "Filipino American" experiences. When I am discussing histories and community conditions and summarizing experiences, I'm highlighting those of Filipino Americans. I'm not discounting all the migrants from the Philippines who became American, however. I'm coming from the perspective of Filipino Americans like myself and my peers, those who were born in the United States or who migrated from the Philippines at a young age. This community walks a thin line between identities that are as different as they are similar—similar to the rest of America due to years of U.S. influence on the Philippines and different because of previous Spanish colonization and traditional Asian values. This gray area makes for a blurred identity that varies in detail throughout the entire Asian American community, but nevertheless contains definitive patterns.

Although I enjoyed every learning moment, I became critical of college organizations and the position of American-born individuals in relation to their family's homeland. This book explores these questions, but feebly answers them as I don't even know the answers myself. Some rhetoric claims that communities recycle narratives and fail to politicize college organizations. How much can American-born individuals be involved, for instance, if we've never even stepped foot in the Philippines? How are we presenting our identity in America? How much do we invest, for what cause, and why? Do we invest at all? I think the answers are simple, but it is also a matter of understanding those answers on an individual level. I am not answering them for you, but, as in a conversation between two good friends, I present the discussion for your consideration.

Along the lines of critiquing our beliefs and actions, I continue to fumble with my cultural identity currently. I find myself constantly surrounded by the Filipino American community I used to avoid, thus minimizing the predominantly Hispanic influence I was accustomed to. Additionally, my stepfather and his family—the Mexican influence that ignited the identity confusion—are no longer in the picture. This isn't a plea for his return because that support system was plagued with toxicity. What remains, though, is the undeniable influence his presence had as I grew up, especially with regard to culture. My relationship with Hispanic culture has shifted because it is no longer environment- or family-based. It has become a part of my past I still hold on to for what it stood for. In a world of political correctness, to what extent am I allowed to claim it as part of my current identity? Do you still define yourself by something, even if it is no longer a part of you? I think we all do. Moments from our past influence who we are now; despite the degrees of separation, there will still be moments when we align ourselves with who we believed we once were.

This book values the middle ground in hopes that those who've struggled as I did can find its words validating and empowering. The gray area exists because so much comprises each individual. We are not completely defined by how we look or our family origin. More importantly, we are not defined by societal expectations of the labels we choose to carry. Though there may be prevailing beliefs that Filipino Americans are supposed to be one way, nonconforming Filipino Americans are not worth less. Each story is unique.

To clarify, this book is my own experience, so it does not speak for everyone. You can change "Hispanic dominant communities" to "white dominant" or "black dominant." You can make my grandfather's relationship into that of yours and your mother's or father's or grandmother's or whoever else embodies home for you. You can change the questions regarding the realm of social justice or disregard them completely. You can alter the details, but the themes will remain—family, identity, culture, confusion, gray areas, and "blank" American. Together, we'll grapple with loneliness, comfort, rejection, discovery, and love. There's something in here you'll know because you've felt it, too. Hopefully, you will learn about Filipino Americans on the way. This book is a beginner's guide to the world I stepped into four years ago. It is a world of self-discovery in the context of cultural identity and is separate from the one I grew up in, yet bigger than I could have ever imagined.

I am handing my heart over to you. It is sensitive and precious. These pages are my life's story and evidence of the conflict I still struggle with today. Identity has recently been a priority in my life and I am still vulnerable and make mistakes in my research. Please be kind. I reference and fact-check as much as I can. I simply hope you'll feel my sentiment within these pages and connect with it on your own. It is amazing how a spoonful of rice can ignite such a journey to self-discovery.

Oh, and did I mention it's all in poetry form? Enjoy.

Love,
Ashley C. Lanuza

# 1

# SPOONFUL OF LOVE

---

Sweet rice hugs
the curve of my spoon.
Its warmth and softness
embraces the roof of my mouth,
feeling like home.
Holding me like you.

## retelling

Hand in hand, climbing up the staircase
lined with blue and gold.
My small fingers clasp tightly
to your wrinkled, spotted palm.
Four in the afternoon and the sun shines.
Warmth and sweetness in our after-school routine,
*let me tell you about my day :*
the books I've been in,
the eyes that laughed with me,
the tribulations I fought.
You listen attentively
pulling out of semi-crowded parking lots.

## nanay gloria's supermarket

Fluorescent bulbs cast a sharp light
among shiny yellow packages of chips and cookies.
The raw smell of dead fish punctures our noses,
as the metal bar of the basket cuts into my palm.
Shouting darts across the market,
*Fried, plea–*
*How much for–*
*Isa nala–*
I watch you speak with people who look like us—
Filipino.
They surround the produce aisles
lined with vegetables, fruits, and
*Chocolate Milk,*
I plead.
You nod your head yes.
It never shakes the other way.

## homework on the kitchen table

If warmth has a smell,
it is bakery-fresh bread rolls.
With deft fingers I pull
the insides of the *pan de sal*,
roll the baked dough into a ball and
flatten it against the roof of my mouth.
Behind me, your wooden spoon hits the iron pan,
causing garlic and onions to sizzle.
They sing songs to my heart
with lyrics of *la-la-la,*
*I love you.*

## dinner at seven p.m. part 1

Brown squares simmer in a sweet-smelling sauce.
I cannot tell if this is cow or pig or chicken,
it all looks the same to me
with potatoes and carrots,
but then is it
*mechado*
*afritada or*
*hamonado?*
It's all the same to me,
good to eat and smell and see.


## dinner at seven p.m. part 2

It is Bitter.
Melon.
My face puckers
like the twists and curves of its skin,
and you laugh because it tastes
like the honey of vegetables to you.
*Just as nutritious,*
just as good for your body, you say,
as you spoon more of the *ampalaya* my way.

## our favorite

Tamarind.
Sour.
Soup.
It looks like potato but isn't.
It looks like spinach but isn't.
It smells like bad gas when released into the air—
twenty-four hours after it is cooked—
but isn't.
Delicious warmth,
comfort well known,
tamarind-sour soup,
you call, *The sinigang is ready!*

## birthday parties

Glass noodles   mixed with *calamansi*.
White noodles   topped with pork rinds and shrimp sauce.
Spaghetti noodles   with hot dogs and banana ketchup.
Thick noodles,   brown and sweet like me.
I slurp,   the pasta slapping my lips,
   sauce covering the corners of my mouth.
I smile,   in anticipation
of the long life you say I'll have.

## kamayan (hands)

Home is made of
    sticky white rice
        boiling sauce, thick and meaty
        sizzling cloves and slices
        humming tea kettles
and the food you've made,
    its steam curling to the ceiling.
Fried fish sits on the table,
    salted and seared
by the market down the street.
Jasmine rice on my plate,
sterling silver spoons shine
beside the fork.
I avoid utensils
in favor of five fine fingers.
Thumb touching
    index, middle, ring, and pinky,
I pick up my rice.
You sit across from me,
mild irritation sprinkled
in your voice as you say
*Pick up your spoon.*
*Pick up your fork.*
*Do not use your hands.*
*We are in America.*

# 2.

# YOUR COMIDA, MY VIDA

The garlic continues to sizzle,
the rice still steamy and sticky,
but there is a change
in our internal residency.
Your daughter finds home in him,
his stature tall and bulky,
not saying *Kumusta ka na?*
but *Hola.*
His tongue sticks to Spanish
and we accommodate his palate.
Your daughter picks up dictionaries,
my ears teach me *Español.*
At least he and I have words
like *basura* in common.

## from sinaloa

*Banda* plays on the speakers and
*chile relleno* sizzles on the pan.
Bags of *machaca* are squished
from a million-hour drive.
It is two a.m. and we are awake,
greeting the family
that is mine by law,
greeting the culture
that your daughter married.

## twisted tongues

The *teleseryes* you play after dinner
penetrates my ears with
drama and murder and love and loss
more exciting than anything from *Days of Our Lives.*
I only understand words to imagine plot,
so in grocery store interactions,
*Do you speak Tagalog?* is replied with
*Hindi,*
my head shaking side to side,
*I understand but I cannot speak.*
*Pero,* in my head I think,
*Sí, yo sé Español.*
When does knowing my Spanglish
take precedent over owning my Taglish?
Why does the latter even need improvement
when you and I eased into English?
My world reteaches my jaw and my tongue,
the crevices and curves of my brain,
the neurons that electrify its thoughts,
to articulate *when not in English,*
*then in Spanish.*

## holding on to what I know

I need Spanish to communicate,
Tagalog becomes fun and games.
*Hindi ko alam* is my only phrase.
*Teleseryes* change into *Telenovelas*.
*Wowowee* turns into *Doce Corazones*.
But every night, the taste never changes
because your love
      for the chopping board,
      the stove,
      the rice cooker,
is endless.
At the head of the table
      glistens the sweet sticky rice,
      meat cuddled by a thick pool of sauce,
all crafted by you.

## three

Hearts hold hundreds of homes.
Mine waved three flags

and didn't know what to do

when everyone else
seemed to just have one.

# 3.

# PLAYGROUND PREJUDICES

---

These are the moments
I did not know were microaggressions,
a result from years of cultural oblivion.
I didn't just learn math or English,
But also that I could be "the other"
Even though Latinos and Filipinos
are more similar than different.

## kids on the playground

They have brown skin,
like me.
They wear red and plaid uniforms,
like me.
They do the sign of the cross before a meal,
like me.
Sweaty and brazen against the sunlight,
like me.
But smelling of rice and *frijoles,*
*rather than rice and you.*

## the little differences

Among other Filipinos, we shared shrimp chips.
White bags that tasted nothing of
Doritos, Fritos, or Hot Cheetos.
Sealed metal thermoses
decorated with pink butterfly stickers and superhero prints,
filled with *sotanghon's* clear glass noodles
instead of chunky clam chowder or red-orange *pozole*.
We share recollections of the market down the street,
seeping with the urgent pungency of raw fish,
stocked to the brim with shiny imported packages.
*They* pinch their faces
expressing recollections
of *their* distasteful memories of the Plaza.

## rice versus beans

The children look similar, but
the cultural contrasts are clear.
They define us, the minority,
as "rice"
and themselves
as "beans."
Kids only twelve years of age,
inflicting
boundaries on the black asphalt,
marked by painted yellow lines.
The girl points at me, *Asian*.
And herself, *Mexican*.

## unchanging

I grow with deep integration because
the stranger-turned-stepfather
teaches Mexican music, food, and culture.
But the girls in the red plaid skirts and
the boys in red polo shirts,
caramel and chocolate skin like mine,
see us as separate.
I understand what they say
and what they share,
but, still.
I am your rice.

## 4.

# FILIPINO CLUB OF ONE

———

Following childhood is
the rollercoaster of changes
in skin pigmentation and texture,
in hair growth and location,
in voice tremor, in my legs crossing, in how I wear a dress,
in who sits next to me at wooden desks,
and who wears plaid uniforms
turned green for secondary education,
and who my true growth impacts and deflects.
Around me I see
brown skin, Spanish last names,
figures against fluorescent light during
"break," no longer "recess,"
and still smelling of rice and *frijoles*.
But I am the only one who smells like rice and you.

## honorary latina

On cold California mornings,
the sun shines on metal benches.
Holes structure the table like a honeycomb,
insecurities persuade my fingers to poke through them.
Laughter rings in my ears,
telling me how I understand but have not *lived*
their family parties,
their protective mothers,
their definition of Latino.
I start to speak,
show that I know
that candy,
      that *banda,*
           *that telenovela.*
But I will never be their "beans."

## one to none

I proclaim that
*I am the Filipino Club.*
I am the only one
    with noodles in her thermos,
     bags of shrimp chips,
      and memories of fish, but no one
to share it with.
I am asked more questions
than I want to answer.
So assimilating comes easier,
muting my differences as if they don't exist,
pushing away being Filipino,
because I was feeling lonely
being the only

member.

## cultural exchange

I trade talks of *debuts* for *quinces* or *sweet-sixteens*.
I trade *White Rabbit* candies for *Pelon Pelo Ricos*.
I trade eating with five fingers for two silver metals,
so that I no longer stand out like a sore thumb.

The crux of adolescence is
how good assimilation looks on me
when it doesn't seem I have much to lose.

## holding on a little less

You are oblivious to my struggle,
but every night, I reconnect
with your homeland
      through the salty, sweet, embracing warmth
      in a spoonful of rice.
And that is enough
on being Filipino.

I am content in our silence
surrounding the subject,
because I no longer
understand what it means,

and I no longer
care to know.

# 5.

# PARTYING PROTOTYPES

---

Dining rooms glow under yellow-orange lights,
    salty *adobo* strikes through the room,
    sweet spaghetti tingles my nose,
       and the sound of crisp *lumpia teases* my taste buds,
enticing nostalgic memories
of every Filipino party I've attended before.
The comfort to my senses is no different.
I hear the murmur of burner fuels,
the curling steam from the rice opens my pores,
my teeth crunch around the lumpia skin.
Silver trays glint under a ceiling fan
and karaoke songs sift from the living room.
The faces and these voices are different,
*family* bonded, not by blood,
but by being godparents at a baptism
or co-workers during a nine-to-five.
Huddled in a corner are gossiping titas,
in another are *titos* drinking *San Miguel*
and a room full of cousins upstairs.

*Hang out with the kids,*
and my parents disappear into the crowd
*as I tiptoe up the steps.*

## nothing i am

I am quiet,
and when asked,
only speak with a tiny mouse squeak.
Fearful of sounding *ghetto.*
Fearful of sounding *white.*
Fearful of sounding *not Filipino,*
as if I know what that means.
I just know that these tropes of
*titas, titos,* and cousins—
are not me.
Not my family.

*Do I belong?*

## lacking experience

My dad's side yells across the room,
        but does not huddle around kitchen counters.
My mom's side makes quiet small talk,
        but does not linger to drink in the corners.
I am the only cousin in my generation
        so I'm left to have grown-up conversations
        as if I were ten years older.
My families are too young or too old
to dance in their Filipino parties.

## sophomore year

Another time in
another room for
another party.
    Gone are the smells of crispy *lumpia*
    or the lingering aroma of *pancit*.

Instead, neon lights
flood the dark banquet hall,
blaring music
eliminates any hope
for conversation.

She wears a large gown
and a tiara around the crown
of her perfectly coiled hair.
Her youthful eyes are masked
with tri-colored shadow.

"15" covers the walls and
her oversized portrait consumes the corner.
A velvet, three-tiered cake threatens to topple,
casting a shadow over the tortillas,
peppers and onions and tomatoes.

In the gleam of the metal serving spoon
hanging precariously over a plate of
steaming orange-stained rice,
I catch my reflection—
caramel skin, almond-eyes, five feet upright.

Then I open my mouth
across the deafening *cumbia*.
The *abuela* raises a brow,
the *tio* opens his mouth,
and the *madre* says, You speak Spanish?

I apologize for my broken grammar, explain
that I learned Spanish for *familia*.
Their smiles sweeten like pan *dulce*—
Here's some more food, mija.

## birthday invites

*Quinceañeras* I've attended: a handful.
Sweet-sixteens I went to: a few.
Debuts I experienced: one.
And it was just mine.

# 6.

# LONGING FOR BELONGING

---

These teenagers
look like me,
speak like me,
and have smelled the raw fish
laid on ice chips.
Then why am I awkward?
*Sinigang, am I right?* I joke.

Silence.

Yet there is warmth
around a culture
I was not born into, but rooted through
because of friends in school hallways
and a distant family not bound by blood.

## missing more than just friends

I yearn for those homogenous groups,
I feel their glances like daggers
as if something is wrong with me
if I don't have a Filipino clique.
With every new friend, you ask,
*Are they Filipino?*
as if it is a standard for acceptability.
Without thinking, I introduce them with
*Oh, and they're Filipino,*
to gain your approval.
Anxiety in identity gang up on me
for what is lacking, whispering:
*Weird.*            Stab.
*Whitewashed.*      Stab.
*Not Filipino enough.*
                         Stab.

## letting go of what I know

I fear judgment.
I fear lacking.
I fear insufficient.
I fear myself.
My fear transforms into yearning
to understand what I chose to ignore.
Dreaming about the Filipino friends
I'm supposed to have.
I am seventeen and my mind thinks,
*I am not rice.*
*Yet I am still not "beans."*
Maybe I am somewhere in-between
or I need to search for what is missing.

# 7.

# COLLEGE-LEVEL DISCONNECT

I am unable to navigate this application.
           In truth, I feel inadequate.
Without Beatrice[1] as my guide,
in the form of money or time,
           I am lost at the entrance of a
twisted America.
I have become my own roadmap
of paperwork and applications,
my own informant.

---

[1] Beatrice Portinari, a fictional character, guided Dante Alighieri towards Heaven in the Divine Comedy (1320).

## your dream come true

I endure sleepless nights
and unending stress
walking a darkened path
towards a degree
that is all we've ever wanted,
so that all your sacrifices
can mean everything.
All *para sa'yo,* all for you.
I marry pen to paper
with my looping signature,
unaware of terms and conditions,
the darkness I will face on my own,
the gnarled growth for me to fully form,
four years of enduring education of the self,
in hopes I flourish
in the Land of Opportunity.

## the lonely road

I wish you could have been there for campus tours.
The world we saw in brochures and neon screens.
I wish you knew what I had to say
when forms and interviewers asked,
*Why, what, and who are you?*
What can I say but that
I wish you could hold my hand
in these moments of introspection,
like you did when there were
rainstorms, crowded streets, a bad day.
Today is a bad day—
the beginning of every day without you.

## not ready to go

*First* in line.
*First* to comment.
*First* in everything.
*First* calls for applause.
Crisp white letters congratulate me as *first generation*
fiery pride courses through my veins—
gratitude for blessings on paper—
yet, for what?
Satisfying starvation with sleep?
Desperately doubting my diligence?
Eroding under education's expectations?
If *first* is supposed to succeed,
why do I fear I have already failed?

## olvera street

Two months living an independent,
college-bubble life,
emptied of Angeleno diversity.
Sitting alone for a dinner plate of
    unseasoned chicken,
        ribs clean of oily residue,
        vegetables grilled without seasoning.
I see black and brown and white bodies
and hear nothing but English.
The only semblance of comfort is when
I take the metro downtown for
    the taste of chile *con mango*
    the blaring of *banda* accordions
    the touch of pink, blue, red, and yellow fabrics
    intertwining my fingers.
The *pueblo* on Olvera Street fills my senses
as I grasp for who I was
before this uncertain reality.
Amid the colorful decoration of
*guitarra* fingers strumming,
    *concha* crumbs littering the table,
and "J" sounds turning into
huffs of "H" phonetics,
I feel at home.

Until I speak
and they call me *Chinita*.

# 8.

# UNIVERSITY OF UNLEARNING

---

New rooms, new people, new start.
So when we list our goals for
*the best four years of our lives*
I decide to seek my cultural identity
in order to answer:
Who        am           I?

## recalling memories

Room of college-aged
Filipino teens,
all bonding over
*titos* huddled over *San Miguel,*
*titas* gossiping in the corner,
and their cousins upstairs.
The air filling with nostalgia
that I do not remember.
My thoughts scream,
*You are not Filipino enough!*
Anxiety digs a hole
and I bury myself.
isolating,
disconnecting.
hoping anyone
will care enough to find me.

## fitting in

Self-isolation in my bunk,
assigned to a room meant for one,
stuffed with three people
on the precipice of adulthood,
Self-imposed anxiety
numbs my bones.
My R.A. senses discomfort,
suggests I attend his student-led class
on *Filipino American culture and history.*
With reluctance I find myself under fluorescent lights,
surrounded by progressive Filipino students.
I act with frigidity, build walls,
afraid of the familiar whisper
*you are not enough.*
I sit through clunky conversations,
then our awkward silence gravitates
towards rambunctious retelling of food–
    sour soup and simmering chunks of meat,
    glass noodles and sweet spaghetti.
Fading away are the disgusted faces
of elementary classmates
when I talked about the fishy-smelling Plaza.
In its place,
nods of nostalgia.

## connecting unavailable

We'd eat what you'd cook if I were home.
We'd sip straws and familiar flavors,
but then narratives would track back
to the prototypes of their family parties
that filled me with loss and longing.
Their images solidify into
> the same drunk uncles on the couch,
> the same gossiping aunties near the sink,
> the same cousins upstairs playing video games,

non-existent in my memories.
*This is Filipino,* I think
*and that isn't me.*
I distance myself again—
different, excluded, and foolish
for believing in a spark of connection,
and realizing this is still not a race I could run.
I am seated at a crowded table,
completely alone.

## presenting convictions

A presentation projection articulates
who, what, and why
is the Filipino *American*.
It does not repeat the stereotypes I hid from,
claiming food as the only indication of culture,
or saying I am just part of the blanket term Asian.
The words instead articulate that I am
a history,
        current event,
                a cultural personality,
an individual with hundreds of years' worth of
power and resistance
sensitivity and shame
pumping through her veins.

## defining the lines

Have you ever experienced yourself
through a textbook?
Because here in the States,
you're worth multiple chapters
when you are a white man.
If you are me—
female, not white, a child of immigrants—
I am barely worth a sentence.
But in these Friday night meetings,
I would read academic articles and essays,
shine a light on *my* missing piece
of America.
The culture I had removed
from every part of my external being
solidified itself in front of my eyes
and I began to see my reflection.

# 9.

# FORGOTTEN HISTORIES

I stuck to the mantra:
*Know history to know self and
no history means no self*[2]
so I dug through a past
not by ancestral linkage,
but by skin color and language and visage,
and a common national denominator—
in spite of separations
spanning centuries and distances.
I imagine their struggles, conflicts, tribulations
triumphs, happiness, satisfactions
in a history not written
in textbooks

---

2   Loose interpretation of a quote by Dr. Jose P. Rizal: "A person who does not look back to where he came from would not be able to reach his destination" or "Ang hindi lumingon sa pinanggalingan ay hindi makarating sa paroroonan."

but found hidden in articles,
>tucked away novels,
>>never-opened presentations
hoping to find a semblance of understanding,
rewriting my definitions.[3]

---

[3] Throughout this chapter, the point of view lens is not my own or directed at anyone in particular. It is a reimagining of historical events through an unknown individual. They are experiencing sentiments common to their particular time and community based on the research available. The accounts I chose are examples of tenacity, grace, and solidarity despite the odds. All histories are referenced and explained in the appendix.

## 1700s – Saint Malo Settlements of New Orleans, Louisiana

Damn these wooden shells,
holding us in blinding and unknown darkness.
We rock back
and
forth.
Taken from our homeland into another land
commodified in the confines of ship trades.
I hear the ocean waves
kiss land that is more alive
than the death chambers we are chained to.
We plan our escape
into the salty-sweet ocean breeze,
carrying the hearts of our ancestors
into territories unknown.
I take a gulp before I drown.
Cold, Atlantic waters attack every wound
on my brown body.
Keep swimming to shore.
Keep fighting for life,
my brothers.

## shrimp paste

Salt puckers my lips but pleases my tongue
with the acidic tingle of shrimp.
Preserved crustaceans grace the Creole gumbo
while Mardi Gras feathers unfurl
against the Orlean ocean breeze.

From the Philippines
dancing with freedom.

Into the Galleon Trade's skeleton ships,
escaping for freedom.

In Saint Malo's
tasting savory, salty freedom.

## 1904 – The Philippine Exhibition in St. Louis, Missouri

*Come one, come all*
*see the monkeys on display*
*in the year 1904*
*at the St. Louis Fair Day.*
We are the tribal ancestors
wearing loin cloths, handmade jewelry,
faces masked with fear and confusion.
Ordered to roast the dogs
of American suburbia,
unknowingly convincing white women
in feathered hats and ankle-length fabrics
that our motherland needs divine salvation
in the form of Uncle Sam.
We are representatives of the country
*Little Brown Brothers,*
performing behind a sign describing us as
Savages
from the Philippine Islands.

## the Philippine Question

With consent of the governed,
imperialism reigns.

Our home is now Sam's little brother
and we will never be the same.

Thomasites, missionaries, democracy, and capitalism.
Lost languages and traditions and the shame of inked skin.

As if Spanish cruelty was not enough,
Americans erase who we could have been.

## 1920s – Migrating Men of Stockton, California

We come to the Dreamland with intention.
Enamored by the picture of America—
purple mountains,
and clear blue skies,
amber waves of grain,
golden against handfuls of sunlight.
Portraits painted
by foreign men and women,
sketching nuggets of gold
lying on the pavement of El Dorado Street.

## just like home

Arriving on buses filled with
tongues in Tagalog and Ilocano and Bisayan.
We float through Stockton,
speaking the language of dreams.
Off the bus, we pass shoulder to shoulder
with familiar caramel faces
to say hello in our dialects—
...*Kumusta*
...Kablaaw
...Maayong
one block of Stockton,
one piece of my Little Manila.

## only golden sunsets

Merciless sun beats our backs
that stoop for hours without end,
nimble fingers pulling at roots
like we pull out our hair in frustration.
Sunset draws near, a few pennies earned.
Lincoln mocks our cracked palms—
*This is your America.*
Upward mobility foretold
disappears with a snap of reality.
The roads we traveled
in California, Alaska, Hawai'i, and in between,
pursuing asparagus, strawberries, and grapes,
all for little nothings.
Gingerly, I place a felt hat on my sunburnt head.
Peering from under the brim I read *El Dorado Street,*
yet I cannot even afford a bowl of *adobo* downstairs.

## the good

Music blasts from the sharply-tuned band and I

throw a week's earnings to greedy fingers and I

grab this woman's smooth fingers into my calloused palms.

Her skin is milky white to my caramel brown and I

hold her tall stature and caress her blonde hair and I

look into her blue eyes trying to find myself and I

cannot find me,

but this is all I have for romance.

## the bad

And I step into the crisp air of midnight

and knuckles grab the lapel of my suit

and my fingers slip from the door

and my head pounds on the black cement—

and I hold my breath.

And their masculine bodies pounce on me
like lions attacking prey.
And their milky white bodies kick mine until
my caramel skin paints the pavement red.

And the crunch of my bones, the slaps on my skin

break me

like the pieces of my already-fractured spirit.

*Go back to where you came from!*
blends with the sound of cracking cartilage
And I scream in silence

because no one wants to hear me.

## the american dream

El Dorado Street
is not lined with golden opportunity
or the Dream I chased.
This world beat me to a pulp,
slashed my wrists and buckled my knees,
disbanded me from my brothers,
raped me of my innocence,
forced me into bed with blood, lust, fear, and shame.
The blue and red lights threaten me—
the suspect of my own undoing,
imprisonment for simply existing,
trapped by an illusion that
America is in the Heart
when the truth is
Pain is the Being.

## exit signs

They grew tired of us
walking their side of Main Street.
They grew tired of us
stealing their jobs and women.

They grew tired of us
existing with our dark skin, flat noses, black eyes.

Paper checks labeled *repatriations* alongside
bags and hats spotted with sweat and dirt.
A paid, one-way ride
in exchange for our promise
to never return
was enough for America
to loosen her grip on our shoulders,
push us back to where we came from
because they grew tired of us,
and my brothers became tired, too.

## empty spaces

Gone was the scent of *adobo*
wafting through Lafayette Street.
Gone was the sound of cue balls
clacking against acrylic.
Gone was the touch of callused fingers
clasping sweat-stained shoulders.
Gone was Little Manila and in it,
a blank space.

## 1965 – Creation of the United Farm Worker's Association in Delano, California

My hands expertly pull crops
in the fields of Delano.
Fields from our *manongs*
still yield plentiful harvests,
though scythes cut down my hopes.
*Enough*
with the low wages under high temperatures,
with the back-breaking work for scant pennies,
with the abuse, the neglect, the pain.

Now,
we fight back.

## please rise

Put your right hand over your heart,

ready,

begin.

Clap, Clap, Clap.
Beat, Beat, Beat

Hands echo
the rhythm of our hearts,
the speed of our movement.

Thunder in my ears,
faster and faster—
we pause.

My left hand outstretched
and my right in the air.

*Isang.*

One.

Bagsak.

Falls.

Meaning *if one falls,
we all fall,
and when one rises,
we all rise.*

Our hearts slam
in unity and community
with our Hispanic brothers.

## united front

We farmworkers
strike against
the fruits of our labor.
Twisting grapevines
acrid as our wages,
yet sweet—
a community built in bitterness.
We stomp the grapes from production
to end the murder of our spirit.

## ¡si, kaya natin!

Cesar Chavez moved
but Larry Itliong began.
And Vera Cruz,
and Velasco,
labor union activists,
eclipsed by an all-Mexican front.
In our reality,
this movement was ushered in
by unsung Filipino heroes.

## 1970s – Demolishing the International Hotel in San Francisco, California

*Manongs* that never left are stuck in America—
home.
Elders sleep in tiny bedrooms—
retirement.
Dinners with men recounting stories from decades ago—
family.
The International Hotel nestles between San Francisco's hills—
"Manilatown."

# the night of '77

**Outside:** "No!"
    **Inside:** The dark of the night fails at masking
        their haunting footsteps
    stomping on the wooden floorboards.

**Outside:** "No!"
    **Inside:** The door knob blasts a hole in the wall,
    words attack my silhouette to *get up and get my stuff*.
I rub the blur from my eyes and fumble for my zipped bag.

**Outside:** "No!"
    **Inside:** The four walls of my home empty,
    bed sheets still warm from my body,
no apologies for the rude awakening I had been awaiting.

**Outside:** "No!"
**Inside:** I see the man I played cards with, the man I drank
          with,
the man I ate with, and the man I cried to.
    They stumble in the darkness,
    holding their livelihood
in cracked leather cases and sweaty palms.

**Outside:** "No!"
Human chains barricade the hotel, shoulder-to-shoulder
        protest
as armed guards carry me from the only home I have,
      from the only family I know.
"Evictions!"

FORGOTTEN HISTORIES

## 1990s to Present – Overseas Filipino Workers

Centuries of Colonization,
Decades of Oppression
have led us to

Years of Exportation,
Months of Tourism,
Weeks of Exploitation
so that I have

Days without You.

## landline

**Child:**
Red and white boxes,
take me back
with your foreign snacks
from another land.
Arabian fabrics,
Italian preserves,
American chocolate.
Paper remittance, cash flow,
tucked in a hand-written envelope.
But none of these gifts replace
the warmth of the bed
when your body gets up in the morning,
the sound of your laughter
when my tiny hands curl around your fingers,
the glint in your eyes
when you tell me you love me.
Come back to me
in the red and white
*balikbayan* boxes.

**Parent:**
Lonely, unable to speak,
left to my own devices on Sundays,
working for meager pay all the other days.
Working regardless of discrimination,
working in spite of abuse,
working not for my survival,
but for a promise to live a better life than this.

## cell phone

**Child:**
Remittances to pay for my schooling,
letters and photos of the days you're living,
while I'm still in this homeland,
dreaming of when your airplane lands
to bring me back *pasalubong*—

to bring you back to me.

                                                  **Parent:**
Always short on cash,
gone in seconds from a written check
in an envelope addressed to you.
Sharing food with other workers
soothes my expat soul
despite the long hours and the long days and the long weeks,
despite mending others' clothes without ever fixing mine,
despite maintaining a home without ever living in mine,
despite caring for a baby without ever holding mine,
despite working for a family without ever seeing mine.
                              I work to put
                              money aside,
                              so that one day,
                              you will be at my side.

# 10.

# COMMUNITY CONDITIONS

---

I am taught that *community conditions* [4]
is an alliteration to define patterns
in our generation.
Conflicts stemming from
*No* from our society,
*No* from our family,
*No* from you,
*No* from myself.

But hearing the Yes of agreement—
that the students around me
heard and felt and saw
and thought the same—
makes me feel less lonely.

---

[4] Community conditions are cultural differences that affect how an individual interacts with their society. Conditions are explained at length in the Appendix.

## hiya (noun)

1. Shame
   > Masks the disgust of mistakes,
   > claiming we cannot risk
   > displaying our wrongs
   > to anyone in our orbit.

2. Save Face
   > For the sake of protecting
   > fabricated normalcy
   > because an individual choice
   > makes all bloodlines look bad.
   > Secrets kept from sight,
   > careful to never tarnish.

3. Sacrifice
   > Selfish wants and desires
   > cannot be acted on when others
   > are in the line of impact.
   > As simple as giving away the last piece of chicken,
   > even after hours of starvation.
   > As complicated as giving up a job promotion,
   > to take care of elderly parents.

Multi-faceted definitions
to avoid humiliation.

## stem

At seven years old,
    two plus two always meant four
        but when it became $y=2x+4$,.
it was a slope I could no longer climb.
    Words like "cosine" and "tangent"
        are a sign my mind would go on a tangent,
    unable to solve the trigonometric equation
that causes devastation.
    You would ask,
        *How was the test?*
I shrug *it was alright,*
even though I broke a pencil and my motivation.
    Still, the back of my head whispers in your voice,
        *Be a doctor, an engineer, an accountant, a nurse...*
        *Be anything but the art in your head.*
        *Be only the numbers on your check.*

## mental

Keep the silence.
If you speak,
then tears should not
fall down your cheek.

Take a deep breath
and let it out—
what are you even whining about?

Chemical imbalances do not exist,
depression is merely a Western myth

because every moment can be fixed
with lips elongated at the width.

## unfair

I can only swim at six p.m.
    when the sun has set.
I can only play outside
    with thick layers of SPF,
        coated as white as they want my skin to be.

*You look dark,*
*You'll get dark,*
*Don't be dark.*

*Morena* pigment covered by
    orange papaya soap
so that my skin glows fair.

Brainwashed by European idealism,
rooted in centuries of imperialism,
direct opposition to the melanin
blessed from sunlit millenniums.

Cannot ignore years of
Chinese, Spanish, and American influence
because naturally lighter skin tones are not a crime.

Yet why is my unfair, opposing darkness
considered tarnishing the rules of beauty?

## utang na loob

Ultimately,
Taking classes that
Aren't going to make you a
Nurse, or a doctor, isn't perceived as
Good enough.

Not in a medical field
Apparently means to go back to the drawing board.

Living my dream life seems almost impossible,
Other responsibilities are more necessary like my
Obligation to give my
Best to a career I don't want

in order to care for you,
who struggled in the unknown.
I work to provide for my family because
their sacrifice brought me here.
It is then my debt to care for
their old age approaching near.

## intergenerational conflict

With voices demanding obedience
no-nonsense, non-negotiable,
parents say,
*You don't have to stay at school past eight p.m.
because in our country,
it was all about the letters on your report card.
You don't have to take an arts class during high school
because where I grew up, math and science mattered the
most.
You don't have to volunteer,
you don't have to dance,
you don't have to sing
because where we are from,
only grades get you into universities.*

But my trembling fists
curl around my crumpled dream
that says,
*We are sorry to inform you
that you focused solely on academics,
which is simply not enough.
Because in America,
you have to do it all.*

## model minority

American assimilation is key.
Assured affluence through
      keeping quiet,
      acting copycat.
Don't disturb the peace—
      don't damage the status quo.
You define protests as *dangerous*
to protect our image
and appease our oppressors.
Only involved in politics
      by watching TV screens
      and circling anonymous ballots,
but faces in demonstrations?
      *Burn the pamphlets.*
Uphold the submissive
Model Minority
to the frustration
of other minority activists.
We are to blame
for our own lack of progress.

## hive

Buzzwords stick to my mind
and sweeten my heart like honey.
I realize my experiences are microscopic copies
of a fifty-state diaspora,
a dispersed culture with more in common
than just ethnic origin.
No longer do I feel alone with the girls and boys,
talking *titos* and *titas*, their parties and cousins.
Hands would raise at every condition mentioned.

Stereotypes do not make me Filipino,
so my palm moves up, too.

## in my silence

These nights wipe away the fog
over the word *Filipino*.
But I keep you in the dark,
separate,
unsure of what you would think.
Maybe it's because
we're a generation apart or
you didn't grow up here or
you didn't attend college here or there.
Or in a "Who Had It Worse" mentality,
what are microaggressions and hidden narratives
compared to your sacrifices?
So I tell you instead about
the subjects I am tested on
the events I attend
and keep quiet about the version of *Filipino*
that grows within me.

# 11.

# IT'S THE LITTLE THINGS

---

In the flurry of exchange
like memes on a Twitter page,
friends and I recount shared experiences—
microaggressions, the little impressions—
unaware that what was said
piled up in my head.
One instance after another
turns me into a face like every other,
a fetish I'm expected to sell,
a piece of food that smells,
an expectation that I must excel,
and a voice I'm told to quell.
All because of who I convey
and how I display,
perpetuated by media fabricated wrongs.
But
I'm not their Miss Saigon.

## birthplace

*Where are you from?*
and I tell my truth.
*No, where are you really from?*
and I respond with honesty.
Aggravated, the woman
throws her hands in the air.
For her appeasement, I reply,
*My parents are from*
and she accepts that as my home, too.
Her insistence communicates:
*You are not American.*
*You are other.*
In my mind, all I know is America.
I don't know *other*.
This question, if directed at you
would have been a simple answer,
while my response required
the invalidation of my being.

## enemy of the nation

A white woman said
I was a disgrace
to the Philippine nation
because I couldn't speak *Tagalog*
to her dog.

## american exotica

He calls me *beautiful*
though we are just talking.
He calls me *fascinating*
even though we've never met.
A month later
in our drunken stupor,
he calls me *exotic*.
We are no longer speaking.

Fetishized beyond repair,
unable to break the image of
Dragon Lady or Lotus Blossom,
mail order bride or war spoil.
Demure and petite and
left to be only a thing
for the undressing imagination.

## "it's not that serious"

It's all the little things like
scrunched up faces at my lunchbox,
divisions as "rice" and "beans,"
referred to as *Chinita*.

Little things that make me
self-conscious
about the skin and body I'm in.

It's the little things
that made me believe I was anything but
everything I have always been.

## to be

Laughter carries through the air,
nods of agreement sway their hair.
Friends and I recount moments when
we were defined as *us* and them.
We have also been
*exotic*
*disappointing*
*intelligent*
regardless of the grades on our cards.
Erasing individuals like an Etch A Sketch,
clumping us like spoiled rice, sticky and wet.
Forcing us to represent billions of lives
by facial structure and the shape of our eyes
When in reality
we are complex beings,
      flawed beings,
      human beings.

## 12.

# COMMON CONDITIONS

---

Other common conditions
not mentioned during Friday lessons
were not always in my narration.
But obvious after moments of observation,
unique to everyone's destination,
thriving in post-colonialization.

## surnames

I am left with only mistakes in my name.
Lacking the power passed between generations
because I remain unaware of origins.
Tell me how to find myself
when I cannot even show them a face
that matches my white first name
and my Spanish or Chinese surname,
or something with too many vowels
for their tongues to twist around.
When I cannot even tell them
to say my name correctly because
I've heard it slaughtered
too many times to count.

## collectivist choices

Family over all—
over happiness
over health
over ambition.
Family conceals all—
conceals abuse
conceals dishonesty
conceals infidelity.
Generations hold on
perfectionism
brought out by suppression
and Christian expectations.
Family perpetuates the image—
light and functional and *normal*.
A picture perfect
toxic family.

## to dads:

Fathers like you only speak in silence
coupled by diaphragmatic grunts.
Other fathers speak in beatings,
vibrations beat the walls
and grow purple-blue lumps.
Some fathers may also speak
through vanilla swirl ice cream cones
or permanent grimaces or
*Don't ever argue with me tones.*
Fathers like you may lecture
but with hesitancy verbalize
*I love you,*
though their hands
and expressions
say every syllable.

## to moms:

Mothers hold our arms
as everything around us burns.
Mothers nip at our ears
to *do this* and *do that.*
Mothers tell us,
*I love you,*
but their actions seem the opposite.
But I love our mothers.
If I could give them the world,
I would.
For all their stooped backs and heavy sighs,
long hours and commuter rides,
then being expected to
cook, clean, and flourish in domesticity.
I'd give them the universe
and more.

## degraded degrees

College-educated in the Philippines,
years and money and sacrifice for education,
only to translate for less on American soil.
Doctors become low-ranking technicians,
famed artists become cogs in the system.
Mistranslations push families into poverty,
but at least it's branded American.
The same fairy tale
sold to the *manongs* of Stockton
hides a reality of
tarnished dreams and broken hopes,
while residing in twenty-first century homes.

## what they won't tell you

*Do good in school.*
I sit at dimly lit kitchen tables,
working on pencil-written assignments.

*Focus on your studies.*
I crumple glossy pamphlets for
honor programs worth six-digit prices.

*We can't afford it, but it's about
academics first, anyway.*
And I get straight As and I study for the SATs
and I exploit my trauma in five hundred words,
yet I am not worthy of thick envelopes
from Ivy Leagues or private institutions.

Acceptances based on grades and activities,
ranking both the applicant and their school.
Yet students have no resources,
no manual for this complicated machine.

Hard work already tainted
by misguided and oblivious choices
in pursuit of the American Dream.

## enforcing expectations

Pulling the corners of their eyes into slits,
excusing all they do with *I'm Asian*.
Filling in gaps of laughter
with their own self-deprecation
only to...what?
Appease the laughter of other kids
that know nothing of us,
but our own fabrication,
regardless of individual complications?
Self-hate in a form of humor,
degrading not only our race
but ourselves,
so that immaturity
becomes our sole accompaniment,
making us all look in poor taste,
killing ourselves in the process
of social assimilation.

## eyes on you

Dining room table gossip
of behavioral assumptions—
*bakla* as if the word cannot be said
under heteronormative pretenses.
Weary eyes on women
    who don't wear dresses,
squinted eyes on men
    who wear heeled wedges,
rolling eyes at the term *non-binary*.
Hiding judgments, forced friendliness,
but behind the curtains, taking the cake
for homophobic commentaries.
Unhappy and afraid to speak his truth
    that rejecting his family is easier
    than admitting his voice doesn't go this deep.
Mad and disappointed in hiding herself,
    that constantly causing conflict is better
    than accepting rejection for who she's with.
Feeling suffocated by the world around themselves,
    that leaving the roof over their head is safer
    than sleeping between walls built by your anger.

## borders

Vexed at their
droopy eyes
and dirt-stained faces.

Vexed at the headlines
of immigrant
separation spaces.

Vexed at myself
because Facebook shares
won't fix broken families.

Naturalized individuals cling to the belief
that their pasts do not follow them,
that *those* people hiding didn't do it right.

Naturalized are still (im)migrants
and if we had a chance,
why can't they?

Fearmongering, prejudices,
our privilege is that we got lucky
within the system.

Inequity for obtaining citizenship,
but fear and pain are equal if you peer
at your mirror image from years ago—

pre-naturalization.
I am disheartened, disappointed at the lack of empathy and action.

## no better

*Model Minority* stereotype overshadows individuality,
but convinces Asians to heighten their superiority.
Within the ethnic hierarchy, even Filipinos are at the low rungs,
and when you say I can't date a black person or
*Why do you look Latina?*
your true colorism is showing.
Race against race,
unable to form unity in the United States.
Pitted against one another by discrimination—
particularly *anti-blackness*—
when it's because of black activists
we even have the right to immigrate.
Have you seen what the system
has done to our eyes?
Tricked by a blinding oppression
to think we are any better
because of our skin color.
Failing to realize we're not white either.
Solidarity only achieved when calling out
the oppression we perpetuate,
in hopes that we no longer
have the desire to assimilate.

# 13.

# REBIRTH

---

My heart holds its breath
in anticipation for the next wave of hurt
over not being taught
                who I am.
Waiting for the wave of anger
over not having sought
                who I am.
Holding for the sadness
over intentionally erasing
                who I am.

## lightning strike

Rumbling Pacific waters beckon me,
*With great knowledge comes great responsibility,*
calling me to hold this history within the veins of my heart,
to contain these insights in the strength of my bones.
Knowledge grasps me in a stronghold—
no longer can I forget, erase, or turn from
the sacrifice, the pain, the lonely days, the empty nights.
It whispers
*do something*
*for your people, your culture, your family,*
*for you.*

I inhale
activism, endurance
power and perseverance.

> I exhale
> motivation, vibrancy,
> courage, and creativity.

## this is filipino

I was twelve years old when I recited
"I Am a Filipino"
by General Carlos P. Romulo.
Rhetoric about inheritance, freedom, and tenacity
was lost on me,
yet my pre-pubescent voice spoke it
merely because of a cultural similarity.

Then I read about me,
and I talked about me,
and I learned about me,
and it became
"I Am a Filipino"
        by *me*.

Redefining identity to include
your sizzling *sisig*,
your tangy *sinigang*,
the *manong's* fortitude in the fields,
the elders' grip in the clasp of policemen,
the overseas workers' four a.m. alarm clocks,
the American-born searching for their reflection
in muddled waters.
"Filipino"
is no longer empty lines or nostalgic flavors.

It becomes a reclaimed    history,
a misunderstood    present,
and an empowered    future.

## broken perfection

A guttural sound escapes me,
anger for the ancestors before me,
though we are not bound by blood.
Intertwined by crimson on the golden floor,
sweating and toiling away from seven thousand islands
in pursuit of a falsehood American dream.

## hesitation

Where you have grown silent with resentment,
I learn the outcry for vengeance.
I'll break these white walls and bamboo ceilings
like they have broken your back and your spirit.
The world hides our truth
because they fear our power
in abandoning their picture-perfect model.
Yet I struggle with speaking in your tongue.
Yet I fail to understand the myths and heroes and histories.
Yet I am not Filipino, but *American*—
upon which battlefield am I validated to fight?

# 14.

# STUDENT ACTIVISM

College organization meetings are
attempts to connect with culture
and like-minded beings.
Projects to initiate community,
Facebook notifications blowing up
from "one family."
Recycling narratives passed down from year to year
of Itliong and Delano and Stockton,
tattooing pre-colonial *Baybayin* texts on their wrists
in an attempt to feel at home in a land
only half of them have stepped in.

## self-led

Evening rendezvous over bowls of *halo-halo* topped with
    creamy purple *ube* melting into
    green and red shining squares of jelly,
    and sweet white beans and soft coconut
sit between me and them.
Speakers prepare for a night of culture and dance
to reconnect with the homeland.
Others rally for annual protests,
demanding reparations for veterans,[5]
a handful announce meetups
with other college organizations.
Blinded by the dark wall projections,
I'm amazed by the large network of Filipino Americans
hidden under my nose.
Going beyond food,
into culture and history and representation.
into knowledge and politics and mobilization,
but active only on the surface.

---

5  In World War II, Filipino soldiers fought under the American flag against the Japanese army. The veterans were promised a compensation valued at almost $3 billion after the war, but the Rescission Act decreased the benefit to $200 million. Many of the veterans have either been partially or not at all compensated. Every Veterans Day, community activists and students rally for the U.S. government to acknowledge the Filipino veterans and provide them their overdue benefits.

## self-investment

Diving deeper in,
until all I see are brown faces,
until all I smell is fried *lumpia*,
until all I hear is bastardized *Taglish*
mixed with caricatures of their parents' accents.
I found exactly what I was looking for,
yet still I feel lost, something doesn't sit right.
Looming in my periphery is criticism for my recycled narratives
because who am I doing it for and why am I doing it?

## self-evaluation

Online captions on Facebook posts
replace photoshoot profiles and vacation shots.
Professional portraits that capture your attention
because of how good I am edited to look.
I ask you to be aware of our issues and histories
in essay-long captions you'll never read.
Suddenly, where I had felt disconnected,
now networks hold up like cobwebs—
I am over-connected.
Empower the youth, retain students,
reuse old workshops reiterating the same narrative,
host annual protests, regional parties,
and explain myself through art exhibits—
*White people grimaced at my food*
and *I didn't grow up with a lot of Filipinos,*
and *I didn't know this history,*
and . . .
        and?
Buzzwords and campus-exclusive methods
to address a cross-continental issue.
Running down the list of internal troubles,
but not getting hands dirty in the homeland.
Parading as Filipino, but not tracing back bloodlines,
whether they flow in the mountains or the sea.
The movement as a whole begs to answer:
*Where do we go with everything it knows now?*

## self-awareness

University activism comes into question when it
delves into modern issues—
from a romanticization of a pre-colonial moment
to a realism of post-colonial struggle.
Wondering,
is it a cultural night or cultural appropriation?
Is it spreading the word of traditions or
perpetuating scripted stereotypes?
Is it investing in a privileged community
or the poor, sick, and lonely?
And at the end of the day, does it even care?

## self-criticism

A bit more politicized,
this university chapter exists to be so lucky
while many across the country
are mostly for socializing.

Yet,
unable to connect,
unable to forgive,
unable to express
how we're truly feeling.

Unable to rally for causes,
against the exterminating and policing.
*That's not our problem, we're American.*

Unable to identify
with people who reflect
the image of our ancestors—
how can we deflect?

Yet,
unable to meet in the middle,
to understand that each has
their own journey,
their own trauma,
their own *beginning.*

How can we ignite a united progression
when we're learning about ourselves
with mixed passions on different levels?

## 15.

# FAR FROM THE FINISH LINE

---

Social media hashtags celebrate *morena beauty,*
a battle that must still be fought.
Viral videos on tasting Filipino food,
opening up the world to our
*ube* and *pandan* and *queso* flavors.
Engrossed in a reiterated conversation about
the same *manongs,* the same colorism,
the same issues without solutions,
repeating into oblivion.
Perpetuating the same narrative
until I've grown tired
from the conversation
and push what I was enamored by
to the back of my mind—
no hesitation.

## lost in one place

Stuck
in this gray area of contradicting
each other on how we should be organized.

Stuck
in this gray area of social activism
and a life without it.
And for what cause?
The American demographic suffers,
but in the oppression Olympics,
we are the lucky ones.

Stuck
in a gray area of movement, unsure
if it's my place to protest
when thrown aside as *not "\_\_\_" enough*
regardless of the books I've read
and the classes I've sat in
and how hard I try
to move away from *just* Filipino food.

Stuck
in questions without action,
as if paralyzed by the truth
that I can actually *do* something.

## finding space

There's privilege in being American,
    despite the hardships and challenges.
        There's a phone call, a letter,
            a position to a policymaker
                in solidarity against human rights violations.
    Prove the narrative wrong
    that those from America don't care
about being Filipino
    unless it pertains to food and culture.
        Still, it cannot be a single concentration,
            when there are still Filipino American rights
            to be addressed.
        Our history remains on our chest,
            waiting to be presented in elementary texts.
    Our rights are gradually failed
by an unimpressive system.
    Multiple battles at different fronts,
        not all chained to *Filipino*—
            there is still the *American* part.

## undo the cliques

Gatekeepers blur the line of acceptability,
forming what it means to be *enough*
as if they hold the golden key.

We're famous for our inclusive hospitality,
yet underneath,
if the individual does not fall into our image,
we refuse to truly let them in.

Every journey varies,
wracked with guilt or refusal or trauma.
Saying,
*There are just too many Filipinos,
I don't want to join.*

They try our spaces,
trying to get a hold of
who we are, but then
*it's too cliquey* and it's true.
We congregate, huddled together
like *titas* in front of dinner plates.

Making them feel *less than* Filipino
when they're barely making the first step—
not everyone on heightened wavelengths of "woke."
Experiences vary, but one thing is certain—
that trying to understand
and a willingness to share
can make all the difference.

## always redefining

I struggle to hold on to my Hispanic ties
that steadily slip from my grasp
as I uncover my meaning of *Filipino*.
But I am still searching for questions unanswered—
What is it like   *feeling Filipino?*
What is         *too Filipino?*
What is         *enough Filipino?*
What            *is Filipino?*
And what do I do with all that I know
about being    *Filipino American?*
In the darkness of understanding,
my grip loosens from who I am at the core
and the lines of my reflection begin to blur once more.

## 16.

# TWO FLAGS ONLY

---

Years of immersion with other Filipinos—
exactly what I sought and wanted.

Yet there sits a hole still waiting to be filled,
unanswered questions adorned with guilt.

Yet there sits a blur of confusion—
whether this tri-question in cultural identity is temporary.

Because I no longer visit the *pueblo* or exercise my *ý* sounds
or sit in the spicy aroma of *chile* rellenos in the making.

And when the *abuela* raises her brow at my fluid speaking,
I say *mama's esposa,* but I do not know how to say 'former.'

I am being and acting and feeling what I wanted myself to be,
as the sound of *banda* accordions fade from the room.

## pueblo

Walking along the Los Angeles skyline,
sunset deep in its hues of red.
The sky stops when I do,
*Hold on.*
And I scan the pinks and blues and blacks
on hand-drawn skulls for *Dia de los Muertos*
reminiscent of days and nights
at the *pueblo* in Olvera Street.
The hairs on my skin stand erect
at the memory of cool midnight air
    as we stood at the front door,
    waiting for bags of Tostito chips
    bursting with neon green packaging,
    anxious to be graced with *chamoy ý limon.*

    And I hear the harsh throws
    of *Español* around the living room and
    awkward smiles in a feeble attempt to
    translate without Google.

        And I feel like I have two left legs
        as the first few notes ring in *El Caballo Dorado*
        and I fumble on the dance floor to go
        right, left, back, turn, trip, fall, laugh.

        And I am pushed back by the
        gust of wind on the 605 Freeway,
        windows down as accordions and trumpets
        blast *banda* about unrequited love.

And those moments are long gone and lost,
and all I have now is a stranger at the *panadería*
to welcome me as *mija*.

## abroad in Barcelona

Bright lights against the black sky outside the diner,
I sit with strangers from Bolivia,
a mother and a father and a daughter.
Spanish words encapsulate their banter with
calmness, warmth, love.
My right arm squished into the metal wall,
I devour the cold *patatas* bravas and
fried chicken wings they've offered,
the crunch replaced by cold, soggy skin.

The mother goads *màs, màs, màs,*
then asks me why I am so silent.
Is it the language, rumbling along so fast?
I shake my head, claiming I was just starving but really,
I felt tears forming at the corners of my eyes
remembering something no longer mine.
Something comforting in my ears
        flooded with a language I stumble on,
something reminding me of
        lockers opening, green plaid,
something reminding me of
        glittering asphalt, red plaid,
something reminding me of
        purple and blue and pink *quinceñeras,*
something reminding me of
        comforting embraces
        that smelled of
        *abuelita's* burnt *frijoles.*

## present

I shove spoonfuls of rice into my mouth,
starving for *my* truth.
I play with a grain between my teeth,
toying with identity,
balancing on the precarious middle of
how much is enough
and if I'm full or if my hunger persists.
Contemplating where I stand
now that one flag was buried in memory.
But, those memories still burst with color
like a mountain sunrise,
gold and gleaming and bright and real.
But, those memories live within me
like the gradient of sunset on beach,
dimming and wavering and sprinting away.
For what can I claim when the family influence
walked out the door?
Now, all I consume is the language and food
and a handful of friends I still stick by.
The identity of my self-constructed
Filipino/Latino/American hybrid,
before this journey into *Filipino-ness*—
      can that still be who I am?
I swallow the grain of rice
like a Dayquil pill,
dry against my throat
and stuck at the opening.
A hard pill to swallow is
knowing that I can now only wave
two flags instead of three.

# 17.

# CONVERSATIONS LOST IN TRANSLATION

―――

Language barriers exist,
not in phonetics, but through vernaculars.
Buzzing in my ears, falling deaf on yours,
spun in political correctness.
But reprimanding you feels silly,
as if a pseudo-wokeness dominates
years of experience and lived-in moments.
Explaining why its *Pilipino* instead of *Filipino*,
when all your life it was Filipino, claimed by actual Filipinos,
regardless of post-colonial romanticism by American scholars.
Rationalizing *Pilipinx* beyond the gender binary,
yet to you, there is neutrality in the original Filipino.

Humanizing a history completely detached from your experiences
and placing colonial trauma through your every act feels like
putting words in your mouth that were never there to begin with.
A reflection of our own inadequacy, our own forced radicalization?
Maybe American-born generations projecting their darkest thoughts
to compensate for years of cultural loss.
I'm unable to communicate
all I've learned, all I've said, the hypocrisy
that the Filipino platform isn't mine to begin with
when explaining what I learned to what you've lived.

## no questions, no answers

Defenses build because our culture states
that obedience reigns supreme.
You are the adult; I am the child.
Respect in keeping silent during your lectures,
nodding my head, agreeing so as to disagree in my thoughts.
Along this wall is uneasy, open conversation,
my questions far more complex than at nine years old—
*from Where did you grow up and what was life before me?*
*to Who are we? Why are we here? And what did it all take?*
Yet I know better than to ask, afraid to open Pandora's box.
*And Why ask?*
you say, referencing the world I live in today.
Free from the same stressors,
from the same heartbreak.
Free from the past I may never know.

## awkward silence

No longer are we walking up the stairs, hand in hand,
from afterschool daycare into grocery store plans.
We sit, facing the television, part of monthly visits.
*How's school?*         Because what else is there to ask?
Yet what else is there to answer besides,         *It's good.*
When *It's good* means I learned about Filipino American history on Monday,
I did a project on Filipino American narratives on Wednesday,
and in hazy inebriation, I discussed Filipino American issues on Saturday.
In my access to higher education, in my ease into English language,
in my privilege of being American-born and raised just as you wanted,
how can I truly complain about how this life is haunted?

## be quiet

In this place,           there should be a quote.
In this space,           there should be a past tense verb.
But instead of anecdotes of dialogue,
I have nothing.
When I want to explain,
    my throat dries up like the Sahara
    my tongue itches like a row of bed bug bites.
Regurgitating simple words is easier
    than calling out your complacency,
    not wanting to disrespect by generalizing you
    as a product of colonial mentality.
Because how does that change anything?
    It won't bring you back to missed birthdays,
    it won't sit you front-row at award ceremonies,
    it won't erase the arthritis or the carpal tunnel or
    the weakened spine.
Work-hard mentality: who cares for social conversations
    when there are mouths to feed?
It only changes me and
    my future, and my passions, and my mistakes,
so we sit           in silence.

## to: me

I am lost in your eyes
not because I'm caught up in the poetics of your heart,
but in your blank stare and unwillingness to share the past.

*We must only thrive for the future, never look back,*
*regardless of who we are and who we came from.*

But that's Filipino, and I am part American,
meaning I am obsessed with the relics of the past
as if they are projections into my future,
enthralled with the belief that my past is everything I am,
otherwise the future is everything I will never be.

## hope and doubt

Maybe all I've learned, read, and shared
you don't claim as yours to begin with
because Filipino *American.*
There is still a difference no matter my angle.

Maybe your reaction does not dominate this conversation,
as we are not the only Filipinos in this diaspora.

Maybe I mobilize to contribute to something bigger,
since this lifetime is not enough for more generations of
silence.

Maybe you do understand what I'm trying to say,
but in your own way, you keep it guarded.

Maybe we can open conversations deeper than
*How is your day?*

And may it be a moment of peace
for all my questions unanswered.

# 18.

# WORK IN PROGRESS

---

*You are enough,*
is whispered into my ears
yet gets stuck at the canals.
I am unable to embrace this murmur.
There is still a list of deep questions—
tiptoeing-the-lines questions
big questions
unanswered questions—
about where our knowledge and activism go from here.
I am still unable to declare
my identity and discovery,
yet confidence lingers behind the curtain of self-doubt.
I write words within these pages, so that the whisper
will stumble through the folds of darkness to find me
and hum my poetry back to me like a nursery lullaby.
Calling to live   within me and hold me and tell me,
*You are enough.*

## awakened

Waking up from a fever dream is the realization
that all I felt and all I thought and all I saw—
I am.

The moments I used to define myself by
are no longer who I am,
yet they still swim in memory,
rising up to catch a breath when called.

The histories written before our time are still me,
because it's a constant battle
to be recognized in the mainstream.

Politicization works through me,
because there's still privilege and power
accessible between the nautical miles of separation.

There is worth in experiences that shape me,
as I write this letter to you,
that all began with
a spoonful of rice.

## claiming

How could I truly explain the gray of painful comfort in the middle?
There is no single molecule, just cross-connected particles.

How could I tell you that I am American—
in my individuality,
my selfishness,
my self-indulgence?
    When I am also Filipino—
    through my collectivism,
    my selflessness,
    my hunger to love.
        And I cannot claim to be Latino—
        yet it remains home in ways
        that I cannot describe
        and that's okay, too.
Walking contradictions, but tell me,
why did I feel so obliged?

## I am

I am not the stereotypes that haunt me at parties.
I am not a model minority flaunting pseudo-satisfaction.
I am not the precarious line of being enough,
       because *I am* enough.

I am our history—
the ship jumpers at the Gulf,
the farmworkers in Stockton,
the activists in Delano,
the overseas workers' *balikbayan* boxes.

I am the Latino influences
that my childhood embraced
with warm *brazos* and *dulce* love.

I am the food you fed me—
       onions and garlic sizzling,
       a bowl of vinegar for dipping,
       chunks of meat in a pool of sauce.

I am a product of immigrants,
your wildest dream, your labor's payoff.
Out of all this,

I am your granddaughter—
and you've made my heart into rice:
familiarity, comfort, home, love.

A love that glows in the cold excuse
of a society we find ourselves in,
where straight boxes and painted lines
force us into unbreakable categories.
A love that moves past these borders
to exchange tender familiarities.

## to lolocon:

I wish I could show you
        Manhattan skylines at sunset.
I wish I could show you
        Parisian lights at midnight.
I wish I could show you
        Belgian waffles, Italian catacombs,
        Spanish villas, Greek Parthenons,
but your tired bones are unable
to tread on cobblestone.
Bones worn by years of work,
only amounting to ominous medical bills.
But to me, your days represent
a chain reaction of sacrifice
all for posterity's better life.
So all I can do is *tell* you
        who I am becoming,
        the words unable to truly paint every color,
        to prickle your skin like every evening breeze.
All I can do is *show* you
        the fruits of your labor
        through shitty Wi-Fi on tiny cellphone screens.
But through the pixelated blur and lagging buffer,
I see sweetness and tenderness
in thirty-two Chiclets
made of acrylic resin and metal
        and I know I've made you proud.

                                              Love, Ashley.

# APPENDIX

## CHAPTER 9

### 1700S – SAINT MALO SETTLEMENTS OF NEW ORLEANS, LOUISIANA

From 1565 to 1815, the Manila Galleon Trade established a trading route between Asia, Spanish America, and later, Europe and Africa. Shipmen from the Philippines worked its decks and research has indicated a number of them jumped ship to escape. Many of these men settled in modern-day Louisiana in their own homogenous encampments. In 1883, a reporter for Harper's Weekly wrote about one of these swamp settlements in Saint Malo. Men lived in homes standing on stilts in the marshy land and were mostly isolated from the cities. These settlements have been washed away due to frequent natural disasters in the area, but it remains that these "Manila men" are "true pioneers [who] have earned a place in the American historical narrative."

**1904 – THE PHILIPPINE EXHIBITION IN ST. LOUIS, MISSOURI**
At the end of the ninteenth century, the Philippine-American war was coming to an end on the battlefield. The Spanish colonizers of the Philippines had signed the islands off to the possession of the United States, but the latter had to decide how to proceed, especially since the Philippines wanted their sovereignty. This was known as the "Philippine Question." The United States devised a scheme—get the approval of the Americans and the Filipinos for the United States to colonize. One of the methods to gain American approval happened during the St. Louis World Fair, a marketplace of technological ideas and anthropological discoveries. The Philippine Exhibition was the largest anthropology exhibit in terms of square meters and featured well-to-do elites and indigenous folks from less colonized regions. The latter were exploited as "savages" and Americans saw the "indecency" of this "tribal" country where people ate dogs and didn't wear Elizabethan clothes. Americans were convinced and imperialism reigned.

*A note: Though these tribes did eat dogs, it was for ceremonial purposes only if no other animal was available. The fair exploited this tradition for the amusement of its fairgoers. Residents near the fair would even send dogs for the groups to eat, despite the ceremony being artificially conducted.*

**1920s – MIGRATING MEN OF STOCKTON, CALIFORNIA**
After an influx of American missionaries and educators began to "civilize" the Philippines, many Filipinos were convinced of the American dream. Moreover, as U.S. Nationals, Filipinos were excluded from anti-migration laws that barred other Asian communities from moving to the U.S. The Filipinos

that migrated in large waves to the United States, known as *manongs*, came in search of the "good life." However, they found themselves at the bottom rung of a social ladder, given the lowest wages, offered limited job options, and suffering intense bouts of discrimination.

Migrants were mostly men who worked the agricultural fields of Hawai'i and the Pacific coast. Certain laws passed by Congress limited the number of female migrants from Asia. In Stockton, California, there was a block known as "Little Manila" where restaurants and apartments attracted the Filipino labor workers moving up and down the coast. After exhausting days under the sun, these men relaxed at places such as pool halls, gambling dens, and taxi dance halls. At these dance halls, Filipino men went out in suits and fedoras to spend some of their wages for a dance or two with a white woman or a white-passing Latina. Many white men disliked these dance halls—as well as the Filipino societies—because they felt that immigrants were taking their women and their jobs. Many Filipinos were beaten for talking to white women; several Filipinos were beaten for even walking on the same street as white men. These moments of discrimination are recollected in *America is in the Heart* by Carlos Bulosan, a Filipino writer detailing his migration experience in Stockton.

After heated complaints from the American public, Congress established the Filipino Repatriation Act of 1935. This act paid for migrants' one-way ticket back to the Philippines. It was an effort to decrease the migrant population. However, not many Filipinos took this opportunity, and it was deemed unconstitutional in 1940.

**1965 – CREATION OF THE UNITED FARM WORKER'S ASSOCIATION IN DELANO, CALIFORNIA**

Filipinos continued to work in the agricultural fields, but as demand increased, salaries remained low, and abysmal working conditions persisted, many farmworkers wanted change. A group of activists, including Larry Itliong, assembled Filipinos on a strike. However, strikers found they were easily replaced by other workers, usually Mexican laborers. In order to establish a more united front, Itliong convinced Cesar Chavez to have the Mexican farmworkers unite with the Filipino strikers. The merged groups successfully gained momentum and eventually became the United Farm Workers Association, a labor union that still exists today. However, after a few disagreements and the lack of recognition for the Filipino farmworkers, Itliong left his position as assistant director. Filipino workers followed suit.

The "Isang Bagsak" is a symbol of unity and empowerment utilized by many Filipino American organizations. The story goes as follows: in 1965 in Delano, California, Mexican and Filipino farmworkers wanted to unite against unfair wages and poor working conditions. To address the language barrier, workers would form a circle at the end of the day and clap their hands into a gradual crescendo, mimicking the speed of the labor movement. Then, they would hold one hand up, palm ready to clap on the other to yell "Isang Bagsak." This phrase translates literally to "one fall," which means that if one falls, we all fall. And when one rises, we all rise.

## 1970S – DEMOLISHING THE INTERNATIONAL HOTEL IN SAN FRANCISCO, CALIFORNIA

Many of the *manongs* retired in the United States. A number of them, along with elderly Chinese tenants, found housing in San Francisco's International Hotel. The I-Hotel was an affordable residence for low-income individuals. They resided in small rooms with a common kitchen and dining area, so many of the elderly came to know each other well. It was a prime place for the retirees, many of whom were bachelors. Anti-miscegenation laws that deemed interracial marriage unlawful were rampant in various parts of the country during these men's prime times. Additionally, due to exclusion acts, there were a limited number of female migrants from Asia. Consequently, many of these *manongs,* who by this time were in their sixties, were not able to establish their own families.

In the late 1960s, the building owners wanted to demolish the living space to create a parking structure. This move was met with vehement protest from the Asian and Asian American communities. Activists held demonstrations for months. However, at 3:00 a.m. on August 4, 1977, 400 riot police were sent to evacuate the building. Despite 3,000 activists creating a human barricade around the structure, police physically removed the elderly tenants from their rooms. In some cases, they used aggressive force if the tenants moved too slowly. The elders instantly became homeless.

The I-Hotel became an empty lot because developers couldn't decide on a sustainable plan for the supposed parking structure. Twenty years later, community organizers worked with the mayor's office to recreate the hotel. By 1997, a contemporary, narrower version of the I-Hotel stood where the original used to be. The original tenants were prioritized during move-in, although a few had passed away after the evictions. The hotel continues to house low-income elderly tenants and a museum discussing the events leading up to the night of 1977. This movement is a testimony to the resilience of the Asian American activist community.

**1990S TO PRESENT – OVERSEAS FILIPINO WORKERS**
Though Overseas Filipino Workers (OFW) was a phrase coined in the 1990s, the phenomenon spanned decades and continues today. One of the Philippines' main exports are its people. Almost ten million Filipinos—and growing—work outside the Philippines. Migrants work in fields like medicine, home care, and tourism, to name a few. Individuals leave their children, spouses, and communities, resulting in years of separation trauma. OFWs typically send remittances—money—to their family members to support their school and housing. Some also send *balikabayan boxes,* shipments filled with foreign sweets, clothes, and toys. Although there is material and financial support, this does not replace the emotional and physical presence of seeing a family member every day.

## CHAPTER 10

Community conditions are cultural differences that affect an individual's beliefs, values, and behaviors. In many cases, Asian culture and norms tend to clash with American society's. Though conditions tend to overlap with other communities, it is this combination of them that makes the Filipino American experience unique. I have experienced most of these conditions. But, I admit that not all the conditions pertain to me and they do not all relate my grandfather, so unlike the rest of the collection, there is no direct person being referenced/spoken to. These pieces represent a majority of the community; additionally, these are the conditions first taught within Filipino American organizations. There are more.

### HIYA (NOUN)

Hiya (hee-yah) translates to "shame." This value is tied to the individual and the family unit. When an individual practices hiya, they are more self-sacrificing, placing the needs of the group above their own. Since family units hold high priority in Asian communities, within the family realm, hiya also means to "save face." These behaviors include not disclosing family issues to strangers so as to not make family members look bad.

### STEM

There is an overwhelming push by immigrant parents for their children to get into scientific fields to become doctors, nurses, or engineers. There is nothing wrong with these professions; however, the push becomes an issue when a child's desires and abilities do not align with these careers and their individualities are dismissed. Most of the push for the STEM field comes from parents' fear their child will not succeed financially. The STEM field tends to provide careers with high demand and a clear pathway.

**MENTAL**

Mental illness and mental health are still stigmatized around the world and Filipinos living in the West are not excluded. The issues around mental illness/health are deemed as almost nonexistent in our communities. Elders typically say to just think happy thoughts to make the negativity to go away. As research has shown, it's not that easy. Due to cultural stigma, the idea of "saving face" (hiya), and other socioeconomic factors, Filipino communities are among the most underrepresented in the mental health care system, especially for long term treatment.

**UNFAIR**

As the offspring of global colonialism and Eurocentrism that dates back centuries, Filipino and Filipino American communities face skin-related discrimination on a massive scale. Like many Asian, African, and Latin countries, Filipinos are told that lighter skin is preferred over darker skin. Products such as papaya soap promise to bleach a person's skin so they are desirable, beautiful, and successful. These products are sold in stores while the media only spotlights individuals with Eurocentric features. At a local level, family members may consciously or subconsciously make comments that discredit darker skin tones. There is nothing wrong with having light skin if a person is born with it. The issue lies in the cultural degradation of darker skin that leads individuals to use damaging whitening products and project these insecurities on others. Colorism unfortunately also perpetuates anti-blackness in many communities.

**UTANG NA LOOB**

Families are central to Filipinos. More importantly, a relationship between "older" and "younger" members is strongly established, evident in terms of endearment for older siblings (*ate and kuya*) and the mano po, a customary way to greet elders. *Utang na loob* is an individual feeling indebted to their parents for giving birth and raising them. This value encourages children to obtain high-paying jobs and, when their parents are older, provide the capacity to care for their parents in their homes.

**INTERGENERATIONAL CONFLICT**

Since many Filipinos migrate to the United States and have children born in the U.S., a difference in values and ideologies between parent and child exists. Filipino Americans tend to cultivate American values that clash with traditional Filipino ones their families enforce. Moreover, American systems differ from those in the Philippines, so many individuals are left to navigate these systems on their own. One prevalent example is the college system. Since many parents attended school in the Philippines, they are typically unfamiliar with the college admissions process and may criticize children for wasting their time on extracurriculars. However, many prominent American institutions expect more than just grades from applicants. Admissions weigh heavily on campus involvement and leadership. There are numerous other values in contention between parents and their children, but overall, these misunderstandings fluctuate in severity and impact.

**MODEL MINORITY**

During the 1960 Civil Rights Movement, white scholars and political leaders grew weary of racial minorities protesting systemic forms of oppression. To combat this, media and politicians deemed Asian communities the "Model Minority," arguing that "all Americans of color could achieve the American dream—and not by protesting discrimination...but by working as hard and quietly as Japanese and Chinese Americans." The model minority became an umbrella term for all Asians, regardless of individual experiences. Throughout the years, this political weapon proved problematic and divisive internally within the Asian community and externally between racial minority communities.

# REFERENCES

Dante Alighieri, 1265-1321. *The Divine Comedy of Danta Alighieri: Inferno, Purgatory, Paradise.* New York: The Union Library Assocation, 1935.

Bulosan, Carlos. *America is in the Heart.* Seattle: University of Washington Press, 2014.

Chang, Benji. "Larry Itliong and Pilipino Farm Workers". In *Asian Americans: An encyclopedia of social, cultural, and political history,* edited by In E. Park & X. Zhao, 577-578. Santa Barbara: ABC-CLIO, 2013.

Fabro, Chrissi. "How to Celebrate Filipino American History Month." FIND, 16 Oct 2017. Accessed October 21, 2019. http://www.findinc.org/findink/2017/10/13/how-to-celebrate-filipino-american-history-month

Hearn, Lafacdio. "Saint Malo: a lacustrine village in Louisiana." *Harper's Weekly,* March 1883.

"History." The I-Hotel - San Francisco. Accessed October 16, 2019. http://www.ihotel-sf.org/history/

Mabalon, Dawn. *Little Manila is in the Heart.* Durham: Duke University Press, 2013.

Matibag, Eugenio. "From the Philippines to New Orleans: Asian-American Creolizations on the Louisiana Gulf Coast." *In New Orleans and the Global South: Caribben, Creolization Carnival,* edited by Ottmar Ette, Gesine Müller, 377-398. Hildesheim: Georg Olms Verlag AG, 2017.

San Juan, Epifanio. "Overseas Filipino Workers: The Making of an Asian-Pacific Diaspora." *The Global South* 3, no. 2 (2009): 99-129. Accessed October 17, 2019. https://www.jstor.org/stable/10.2979/gso.2009.3.2.99

Sit, Michelle. "The Filipino 'exhibit' at the 1904 St. Louis World's Fair, Missouri." *Santa Cruz Report,* 2, (2008).

Agbayani-Siewert, Pauline. "Filipino American Culture and Family: Guidelines for Practitioners." *Families in Society: The Journal of Contemporary Human Services,* no. 44 (1994): 429-438.

Chou, Rosalind and Joe Feagin. "Myth of the Model Minority: Asian Americans facing racism." Boulder: Paradigm Publishers, 2008.

Hunter, Margaret. "The Persistent Problem of Colorism: Skin Tone, Status, and Inequality." *Sociology Compass* 10, no. 1 (2007), 237-254.

Sanchez, Francis and Albert Gaw. "Mental Health Care of Filipino Americans." *Psychiatric Services* 58, no. 6 (2007), 810-815.

Uhm, Soo Yun. "Factors Influencing Chinese and Filipino American College Students' Stereotypical Major and Occupation." PhD diss., University of California Santa Barbara, 2004.

Ying, Yu-Wen. "The Effect of Intergenerational Conflict and School-Based Racial Discrimination and Academic Achievement in Filipino American Adolescents." *Journal of Immigrant and Refugee Studies* 4, no. 4 (2006), 19-35.

Klein, Christopher. "Filipino Americans Fought With U.S. in WWII, Then Had to Fight for Veterans Benefits." History, 11 Nov 2019. Accessed October 21, 2019. https://www.history.com/news/filipino-americans-veterans-day

# ACKNOWLEDGEMENTS

---

Writing a draft may take a person or two, but publishing a book takes a village. I am beyond grateful for each individual who has invested a part of themselves in the realization of this dream.

I'd like to first thank God for every blessing He has placed my way.

Thank you, Lolocon, for being the center of this collection through your cooking, your wisdom, and your love. Thank you, Mom, for the sacrifices in your personal life, for your inspiring strength I wish I had, and for caring for me more than I deserve. Thank you, Dad, for those talks sitting in traffic on Friday night, doing your best to support all I do, and making me laugh so hard, I have two large dimples. Thank you, Tita Sep, for inspiring me to be where I am today, pushing me to always do better, and challenging me constantly. Thank you to my little brothers—Markito, Angelo, and Alexander—for giving me the joy of being your older sister. I hope this book can serve as a guide when ya'll grow up. Thank you, Jason, for acting as a role model and pushing me toward my potential. Thank you, Mommy Susan and Uncle Neil, for being so uplifting, loving, and firm believers in my dreams. Thank you, Lola Linda, for your constant matronly support. I hope I've made you and Nono proud. Thank you to the Lanuza, Cariasa, Lau, Sunglao, Rea, Santillan, Ticzon, Raygoza, Dee, Choomngern, and Abaya families for the constant affirmations since this writing journey began. Also, thank you to my dog, Lucky. I appreciate all of you.

Thank you, Mia, for reading my poetry since day one. We've seen so much of each other's lives and I'm so thankful for our friendship. Thank you to Michelle and Barbara, who knew me before UCLA and still schedule time together despite our distances. I couldn't have understood so much of who I am without ya'll. Thank you to my amazing Bruin support system—Gaby, Allaine, Maria, Lilybeth, Andrea, Collin, and Justin. And, of course, my Fab Five—Justeen, Jasmine, Emily, and Amber. Thank you to each of you for being a shoulder to cry on, someone to bounce an idea off of, a passenger on my late-night drives, and motivation during study sessions. Ya'll are the best. Thank you, Edward, for being my best friend and my #2 fan. I'm so grateful for you.

Huge thanks to Samahang Pilipino and my mentors who taught me so much about being a writer and a Pinay. Thank you, Jo Anne, Marielle, Laura, Kevin, Maurus, Paul, Mariah, Valerie, Andrew, and Kristine. I am constantly in awe of your energy and inspired by everything you stand for. Also, thank you to Professor Matsumoto, Teresa, Andrew, Kevin, Allaine, and Justeen for taking the time to help with revisions. Special acknowledgement to the legacies of Carlos Bulosan and

Dr. Dawn Mabalon for sparking my passion for expressing my Filipino American identity.

I want to extend my appreciation to St. Bernard's, San Gabriel Mission's, and UCLA's faculty, staff, and communities for making me the writer I am today. Also, thank you to the European interrail train system and Leiden University College for providing me a home during the nitty gritty of revisions.

Thank you to the publishing team at New Degree Press! Special thanks to Eric, Brian, Jennifer, Elina, Kara, and Liana for making my dreams come true. I definitely couldn't have done this without ya'll.

Thank you to everyone who supported the pre-order campaign. Shoutout to Jeffrey Rirao, Joseph Gomez, Jocelyn Vibar, Sarahmae Natividad, Earl Torres, Bethanie Arucan, Ita Gonzalez, Erin Weir, Edgardo and Theresa Cruz, Richard Alarcon, Shari Ginsberg, Ariel Lanuza, Armida Lanuza, Theresa Trieu, Rachel Gallardo, Khayman McDaniels, Julianne Dinsay, Joybelle Naigan, Margaret Von Rotz, Michaela Serafica, Christian Torres, Norma Mallorca, Joanna Yang, Charles Choomngern, Gabrielle Morales, Karen Choup, Carissa Payongayong, Lance Alviso, Alethiea Taylor, Kent Marume, Jacklyn Lozada, Preciosa Alacar, Alyssa Moreno, Luke Apodaca, John Peradilla, Kathleen Vidanes, Rummel Requerme, Jamie Dela Cruz, Alma Stone, Juny Nguyen, Markee Mendez, Jhoanna Gatchalian, Angela Mastantuono, Joemarc Sunglao, Steffi Sibal, Elijah Tolentino, Earl Lozada, Chynna Porrata, Ellen Renskoff, Maria Hammett, Michael Estabillo, Matt Ferrer, Leo Albea, Zinnia Arcinue, Zeila

Vicente, Aimiel Casillan, Shiroëlla Lancelot, Daisha Dominic, Crystal Vine, Larry Laboe, Eugenie Heilweil, Angel Barajas, Jason Salvador Wenceslao, Jr., Kristen Connors, Kristine Ocampo, Ashra Tugung, Angel Trazo, Vanessa Codilla, and Michelle Borabo. And special thanks to SGMHS, the Ginsbergs, Alice Chi, Valerie Matsumoto, and Danielle Dina.

Finally, thank you to everyone who gave me advice, clarity, support, and assistance with spreading the word and gathering amazing momentum to publish a book I am proud of. And for anyone I didn't list, know I am sincerely grateful for you, too.

We did it!

*Love,*
*Ashley C. Lanuza*

Made in the USA
Las Vegas, NV
23 May 2022